I0753425

The New Poetry Series

PUBLISHED BY

HOUGHTON MIFFLIN COMPANY

IRRADIATIONS. SAND AND SPRAY. JOHN GOULD FLETCHER.

SOME IMAGIST POETS.

JAPANESE LYRICS. Translated by LAFCADIO HEARN.

AFTERNOONS OF APRIL. GRACE HAZARD CONKLING.

THE CLOISTER: A VERSE DRAMA. EMILE VERHAEREN.

INTERFLOW. GEOFFREY C. FABER.

STILLWATER PASTORALS AND OTHER POEMS. PAUL SHIVELL.

IDOLS. WALTER CONRAD ARENSBERG.

TURNS AND MOVIES, AND OTHER TALES IN VERSE. CONRAD AIKEN.

ROADS. GRACE FALLOW NORTON.

GOBLINS AND PAGODAS. JOHN GOULD FLETCHER.

SOME IMAGIST POETS, 1916.

A SONG OF THE GUNS. GILBERT FRANKAU.

GOBLINS AND PAGODAS

GOBLINS AND PAGODAS

BY

JOHN GOULD FLETCHER

BOSTON AND NEW YORK
HOUGHTON MIFFLIN COMPANY
The Riverside Press Cambridge
1916

Published April 1916

TO

DAISY

THANKS are due to the editor of The Egoist, London, for permission to reprint The Ghosts of an Old House and the Orange Symphony; to the editor of Poetry, Chicago, for permission to reprint the Blue Symphony; and to the editor of The Little Review for permission to reprint the Green Symphony.

PREFACE

I

THE second half of the nineteenth and the first fifteen years of the twentieth century have been a period of research, of experiment, of unrest and questioning. In science and philosophy we have witnessed an attempt to destroy the mechanistic theory of the universe as developed by Darwin, Huxley, and Spencer. The unknowable has been questioned: hypotheses have been shaken: vitalism and idealism have been proclaimed. In the arts, the tendency has been to strip each art of its inessentials and to disclose the underlying basis of pure form. In life, the principles of nationality, of racial culture, of individualism, of social development, of Christian ethics, have been discussed, debated, and examined from top to bottom, until at last, in the early years of the twentieth century we find all Europe, from the leaders of thought down to the lowest peasantry, engaged in a mutually destructive war of which few can trace the beginnings and none can foresee the end. The fundamental tenets of thought, art, life itself, have been shaken: and either civilization is destined to some new birth, or mankind will revert to the conditions of life, thought, and social intercourse that prevailed in the Stone Age.

PREFACE

Like all men of my generation, I have not been able to resist this irresistible upheaval of ideas and of forces: and, to the best of my ability, I have tried to arrive at a clear understanding of the fundamentals of æsthetic form as they affect the art to which I have felt myself instinctively akin, the art of poetry. That I have completely attained such an understanding, it would be idle for me to pretend: but I believe, and have induced some others to believe, that I have made a few steps towards it. Some explanation of my own peculiar theories and beliefs is necessary, however, to those who have not specifically concerned themselves with poetry, or who suffer in the presence of any new work of art from the normal human reaction that all art principles are so essentially fixed that any departure from accepted ideas is madness.

II

The fundamental basis of all the arts is the same. In every case art aims at the evocation of some human emotion in the spectator or listener. Where science proceeds from effects to causes, and seeks to analyze the underlying causes of emotion and sensation, art reverses the process, and constructs something that will awaken emotions, according to the amount of receptiveness with which other people approach it. Thus architecture gives us feelings of density, proportion, harmony: sculpture, of masses in movement;

painting, of colour-harmony and the ordered composition of lines and volumes from which arise sensations of space: music, of the development of sounds into melodic line, harmonic progression, tonal opposition, and symphonic structure.

The object of literature is not dissimilar from these. Literature aims at releasing the emotions that arise from the formed words of a certain language. But literature is probably a less pure — and hence more universal — art than any I have yet examined. For it must be apparent to all minds that not only is a word a definite symbol of some fact, but also it is a thing capable of being spoken or sounded. The art of literature, then, in so far as it deals with definite statements, is akin to painting or photography: in so far as it deals with sounded words, it is akin to music.

III

Literature, therefore, does not depend on the peculiar twists and quirks which represent, to those who can read, the words, but rather on the essential words themselves. In fact, literature existed before writing; and writing in itself is of no value from the purely literary sense, except in so far as it preserves and transmits from generation to generation the literary emotion. Style, whether in prose or poetry, is an attempt to develop this essentially musical quality of literature, to evoke the magic that exists in the sound-quality of words, as well as to combine these sound-qualities in definite statements or sentences. The difference between prose and poetry is, therefore, not a difference of means, but of psychological effect and reaction. The means employed, the formed language, is the same: but the resultant impression is quite different.

In prose, the emotions expressed are those that are capable of development in a straight line. In so far as prose is pure, it confines itself to the direct orderly progression of a thought or conception or situation from point to point of a flat surface. The sentences, as they develop this conception from its beginning to conclusion, move on, and do not return upon themselves. The grouping of these sentences into paragraphs gives the breadth of the thought. The paragraphs, sections, and chapters are each a square, in that they represent a division of the main thought into parallel units, or blocks of subsidiary ideas. The sensation of depth is finally obtained by arranging these blocks in a rising climacteric progression, or in parallel lines, or in a sort of zigzag figure.

The psychological reaction that arises from the intelligent appreciation of poetry is quite different. In poetry, we have a succession of curves. The direction of the thought is not in straight lines, but wavy and spiral. It rises and falls on gusts of strong emotion. Most often it creates strongly marked loops and circles. The structure of the stanza or strophe always tends to the spherical. Depth is obtained by making one sphere contain a number of concentric, or overlapping spheres.

Hence, when we speak of poetry we usually mean regular rhyme and metre, which have for so long been considered essential to all poetry, not as a device for heightening musical effect, as so many people suppose, but merely to make these loops and circles more accentuated, and to make the line of the poem turn upon itself more recognizably. But it must be recognized that just as Giotto's circle was none the less a circle, although not drawn with compasses, so poetic circles can be constructed out of subtler and more musical curves than that which painstakingly follows the selfsame progression of beats, and catches itself up on the same point of rhyme for line after line. The key-pattern on the lip of a Greek vase may be beautiful, but it is less beautiful, less satisfying, and less conclusive a test of artistic ability than the composition of satyrs and of mænads struggling about the centre. Therefore I maintain, and will continue to do so, that the mere craftsman-ability to write in regular lines and metres no more makes a man a poet than the ability to stencil wall-papers makes him a painter.

Rather is it more important to observe that almost any prose work of imaginative literature, if examined closely, will be found to contain a plentiful sprinkling of excellent verses; while many poems which the world hails as masterpieces, contain whole pages of prose. The fact is, that prose and poetry are to literature as composition and colour are to painting, or as light and shadow to the day, or male and female to mankind. There are no absolutely perfect poets and no absolutely perfect prose-writers. Each partakes of some of the characteristics of the other. The difference between poetry and prose is, therefore, a difference between a general roundness and a general squareness of outline. A great French critic, recently dead, who devoted perhaps the major part of his life to the study of the æsthetics of the French tongue, declared that Flaubert and Chateaubriand wrote only poetry. If there are those who cannot see that in the only true and lasting sense of the word poetry, this remark was perfectly just, then all I have written above will be in vain.

IV

Along with the prevailing preoccupation with technique which so marks the early twentieth century, there has gone also a great change in the subject-matter of art. Having tried to explain the æsthetic form-basis of poetry, I shall now attempt to explain my personal way of viewing its content.

It is a significant fact that every change in technical procedure in the arts is accompanied by, and grows out of, a change in subject-matter. To take only one out of innumerable examples, the new subject-matter of Wagner's music-dramas, of an immeasurably higher order than the usual libretto, created a new form of music, based on motifs, not melodies. Other examples can easily be discovered. The reason for this is not difficult to find.

No sincere artist cares to handle subject-matter that has already been handled and exhausted. It is not a question of a desire to avoid plagiarism, or of self-conscious searching for novelty, but of a perfectly spontaneous and normal appeal which any new subject-matter always makes. Hence, when a new subject appears to any artist, he always realizes it more vividly than an old one, and if he is a good artist, he realizes it so vividly that he re-creates it in what is practically a novel form.

This novel form never is altogether novel, nor is the subject altogether a new subject. For, as I pointed out at the beginning of this preface, that all arts sprang practically out of the same primary sensations, so the subject-matter of all art must forever be the same: namely, nature and human life. Hence, any new type of art will always be found, in subject-matter as well as in technique, to have its roots in the old. Art is like a kaleidoscope, capable of many changes, while the material which builds up those changes remains the same.

Nevertheless, although the subject-matter in this book is not altogether new, yet I have realized it in a way which has not often been tried, and out of that fresh and quite personal realization have sprung my innovations in subject as well as technique. Let me illustrate by a concrete example.

V

A book lies on my desk. It has a red binding and is badly printed on cheap paper. I have had this book with me for several years. Now, suppose I were to write a poem on this book, how would I treat the subject?

If I were a poet following in the main the Victorian tradition, I should write my poem altogether about the contents of this book and its author. My poem would be essentially a criticism of the subject-matter of the book. I should state at length how that subject-matter had affected me. In short, what the reader would obtain from this sort of poem would be my sentimental reaction towards certain ideas and tendencies in the work of another.

If I were a realist poet, I should write about the book's external appearance. I should expatiate on the red binding, the bad type, the ink-stain on page sixteen. I should complain, perhaps, of my poverty at not being able to buy a better edition, and conclude with a gibe at the author for not having realized the sufferings of the poor.

Neither of these ways, however, of writing about this book possesses any novelty, and neither is essentially my own way. My own way of writing about it would be as follows:—

I should select out of my life the important events connected with my ownership of this book, and strive to write of them in terms of the volume itself, both as regards subject-matter and appearance. In other words, I should link up my personality and the personality of the book, and make each a part of the other. In this way I should strive to evoke a soul out of this piece of inanimate matter, a something characteristic and structural inherent in this inorganic form which is friendly to me and responds to my mood.

This method is not new, although it has not often been used in Occidental countries. Professor Fenollosa, in his book on Chinese and Japanese art, states that it was universally employed by the Chinese artists and poets of the Sung period in the eleventh century A.D. He calls this doctrine of the interdependence of man and inanimate nature, the cardinal doctrine of Zen Buddhism. The Zen Buddhists evolved it from the still earlier Taoist philosophy, which undoubtedly inspired Li Po and the other great Chinese poets of the seventh and eighth centuries A.D.

VI

In the first poems of this volume, the "Ghosts of an Old House," I have followed the method already described. I have tried to evoke, out of the furniture and surroundings of a certain old house, definite emotions which I have had concerning them. I have tried to relate my childish terror concerning this house — a terror not uncommon among children, as I can testify — to the aspects that called it forth.

In the "Symphonies," which form the second part of this volume, I have gone a step further. My aim in writing these was, from the beginning, to narrate certain important phases of the emotional and intellectual development — in short, the life — of an artist, not necessarily myself, but of that sort of artist with which I might find myself most in sympathy. And here, not being restrained by any definite material phenomena, as in the Old House, I have tried to state each phase in the terms of a certain colour, or combination of colours, which is emotionally akin to that phase. This colour, and the imaginative phantasmagoria of landscape which it evokes, thereby creates, in a definite and tangible form, the dominant mood of each poem.

The emotional relations that exist between form, colour, and sound have been little investigated. It is perfectly true that certain colours affect certain temperaments differently. But it is also true that there is a science of colour, and that certain of its laws are already universally known, if not explained. Naturally enough, it is to the painters we must first turn if we want to find out what is known about colour. We discover that painters continually are speaking of hot and cold colour: red, yellow, orange being generally hot, and green, blue, and violet cold — mixed colours being classed hot and cold according to the proportions they contain of the hot and cold colours. We also discover that certain colours will not fit certain forms, but rebel at the combination. This is so far true that scarcely any landscape painter finishes his pictures from nature, but in the studio: and almost any art student, painting a landscape, will disregard the colour before him and employ the colour-scheme of his master or of some painter he admires. As Delacroix noted in his journal: "A conception having become a composition must move in the milieu of a colour peculiar to it. There seems to be a particular tone belonging to some part of every picture which is a key that governs all the other tones."

Therefore, we must admit that there is an intimate relation between colour and form. It is the same with colour and sounds. Many musicians have observed the phenomenon, that when certain notes, or combinations of them, are sounded, certain colours are also suggested to the eye. A Russian composer, Scriabine, went so far as to construct colour-scales, and an English scientist, Professor Wallace Rimington, has built an organ which plays in colours, instead of notes. Unfortunately, the musicians have given this subject less attention than the painters, and therefore our knowledge concerning the relations of colour and sound is more fragmentary and incomplete. Nevertheless, these relations exist, and it is for the future to develop them more fully.

Literature, and especially poetry, as I have already pointed out, partakes of the character of both painting and music. The impressionist method is quite as applicable to writing as it is to landscape. Poems can be written in major or minor keys, can be as full of dominant motif as a Wagner music-drama, and even susceptible of fugal treatment. Literature is the common ground of many arts, and in its highest development, such as the drama as practised in fifth-century Athens, is found allied to music, dancing, and colour. Hence, I have called my works "Symphonies," when they are really dramas of the soul, and hence, in them I have used colour for verity, for ornament, for drama, for its inherent beauty, and for intensifying the form of the emotion that each of these poems is intended to evoke.

VII

Let us take an artist, a young man at the outset of his career. His years of searching, of fumbling, of other men's influence, are coming to an end. Sure of himself, he yet sees that he will spend all his life pursuing a vision of beauty which will elude him at the very last. This is the first symphony, which I have called the "Blue," because blue suggests to me depth, mystery, and distance.

He finds himself alone in a great city, surrounded by

noise and clamour. It is as if millions of lives were tugging at him, drawing him away from his art, tempting him to go out and whelm his personality in this black whirlpool of struggle and failure, on which float golden specks — the illusory bliss of life. But he sees that all this is only another illusion, like his own. Here we have the "Symphony in Black and Gold."

He emerges from the city, and in the country is re-intoxicated with desire for life by spring. He vows himself to a self-sufficing pagan worship of nature. This is the "Green Symphony."

Quickened by spring, he dreams of a marvellous golden city of art, full of fellow-workers. This city appears to him at times like some Italian town of the Renaissance, at others like some strange Oriental golden-roofed monastery-temple. He sees himself dead in the desert far away from it. Yet its blossoming is ever about him. Something divine has been born of him after death.

So he passes to the "White Symphony," the central poem of this series, in which I have sought to describe the artist's struggle to attain unutterable and superhuman perfection. This struggle goes on from the midsummer of his life to midwinter. The end of it is stated in the poem.

There follows a brief interlude, which I have called a "Symphony in White and Blue." These colours were chosen perhaps more idiosyncratically in this case than in the others. I have tried to depict the sort of temptation that besets most artists at this stage of their career: the temptation to abandon the struggle for the sake of a purely sensual existence. In this case, however, the appeal of sensuality is conveyed under the guise of a dream. It is resisted, and the struggle begins anew.

War breaks out, not alone in the external world, but in the artist's soul. He finds he must follow his personality wherever it leads him, despite all obstacles. This is the "Orange Symphony."

Now follow long years of struggle and neglect. He is shipwrecked, and still afar he sees his city of art, but this time it is red, a phantom mocking his impotent rage.

Old age follows. All is violet, the colour of regret and remembrance. He is living only in the past, his life a succession of dreams.

Lastly, all things fade out into absolute grey, and it is now midwinter. Looking forth on the world again he still sees war, like a monstrous red flower, dominating mankind. He hears the souls of the dead declaring that they, too, have died for an adventure, even as he is about to die.

Such, in the briefest possible analysis, is the meaning of the poems contained in this book.

January, 1916.

CONTENTS

CONTENTS

CONTENTS

SECTION I

THE GHOSTS OF AN OLD HOUSE

PROLOGUE

THE house that I write of, faces the north:
No sun ever seeks
Its six white columns,
The nine great windows of its face.

It fronts foursquare the winds.

Under the penthouse of the veranda roof,
The upper northern rooms
Gloom outwards mournfully.

Staring Ionic capitals
Peer in them:
Owl-like faces.

On winter nights
The wind, sidling round the corner,
Shoots upwards
With laughter.

The windows rattle as if some one were in them
wishing to get out
And ride upon the wind.

THE GHOSTS OF AN OLD HOUSE

Doors lead to nowhere:
Squirrels burrow between the walls.
Closets in every room hang open,
Windows are stared into by uncivil ancient trees.

In the middle of the upper hallway
There is a great circular hole
Going up to the attic.
A wooden lid covers it.

All over the house there is a sense of futility;
Of minutes dragging slowly
And repeating
Some worn-out story of broken effort and desire.

PART I. THE HOUSE

BEDROOM

THE clump of jessamine
Softly beneath the rain
Rocks its golden flowers.

In this room my father died:
His bed is in the corner.
No one has slept in it
Since the morning when he wakened
To meet death's hands at his heart.
I cannot go to this room,
Without feeling something big and angry
Waiting for me
To throw me on the bed,
And press its thumbs in my throat.

The clump of jessamine
Without, beneath the rain,
Rocks its golden flowers.

THE HOUSE

LIBRARY

Stuffy smell of mouldering leather,
Tattered arm-chairs, creaking doors,
Books that slovenly elbow each other,
Sown with children's scrawls and long
Worn out by contact with generations:
Tattered tramps displaying yourselves —
"We, though you broke our backs, did not complain."
If I had my way,
I would take you out and bury you quickly,
Or give you to the clean fire.

INDIAN SKULL

Some one dug this up and brought it
To our house.
In the dark upper hall, I see it dimly,
Looking at me through the glass.

Where dancers have danced, and weary people
Have crept to their bedrooms in the morning,
Where sick people have tossed all night,
Where children have been born,
Where feet have gone up and down,
Where anger has blazed forth, and strange looks
have passed,

THE GHOSTS OF AN OLD HOUSE

It has rested, watching meanwhile
The opening and shutting of doors,
The coming and going of people,
The carrying out of coffins.

Earth still clings to its eye-sockets,
It will wait, till its vengeance is accomplished.

OLD NURSERY

In the tired face of the mirror
There is a blue curtain reflected.
If I could lift the reflection,
Peer a little beyond, I would see
A boy crying
Because his sister is ill in another room
And he has no one to play with:
A boy listlessly scattering building blocks,
And crying,
Because no one will build for him the palace of
Fairy Morgana.
I cannot lift the curtain:
It is stiff and frozen.

THE HOUSE

THE BACK STAIRS

In the afternoon
When no one is in the house,
I suddenly hear dull dragging feet
Go fumbling down those dark back stairs,
That climb up twisting,
As if they wanted no one to see them.
Beating a dirge upon the bare planks
I hear those feet and the creak of a long-locked door.

My mother often went
Up and down those selfsame stairs,
From the room where by the window
She would sit all day and listlessly
Look on the world that had destroyed her,
She would go down in the evening
To the room where she would sleep,
Or rather, not sleep, but all night
Lie staring fiercely at the ceiling.

In the afternoon
When no one is in the house:
I suddenly hear dull dragging feet
Beating out their futile tune,
Up and down those dark back stairs,
But there is no one in the shadows.

THE GHOSTS OF AN OLD HOUSE

THE WALL CABINET

Above the steep back stairs
So high that only a ladder can come to it,
There is a wall cabinet hidden away.

No one ever unlocks it;
The key is lost, the door is barred,
It is shut and still.

Some say, a previous tenant
Filled its shelves with rows of bottles,
Bottles of spirit, filled with spiders.

I do not know.
Above the sleepy still back stairs,
It watches, shut and still.

THE CELLAR

Faintly lit by a high-barred grating,
The low-hung cellar,
Flattens itself under the house.

In one corner
There is a little door,
So low, it can scarcely be seen.

THE HOUSE

Beyond,
There is a narrow room,
One must feel for the walls in the dark.

One shrinks to go
To the end of it,
Feeling the smooth cold wall.

Why did the builders who made this house,
Stow one room away like this?

THE FRONT DOOR

It was always the place where our farewells were taken,
When we travelled to the north.

I remember there was one who made some journey,
But did not come back.
Many years they waited for him,
At last the one who wished the most to see him,
Was carried out of this selfsame door in death.

Since then all our family partings
Have been at another door.

PART II. THE ATTIC

IN THE ATTIC

DUST hangs clogged so thick
The air has a dusty taste:
Spider threads cling to my face,
From the broad pine-beams.
There is nothing living here,
The house below might be quite empty,
No sound comes from it.
The old broken trunks and boxes,
Cracked and dusty pictures,
Legless chairs and shattered tables,
Seem to be crying
Softly in the stillness
Because no one has brushed them.
No one has any use for them, now,
Yet I often wonder
If these things are really dead:
If the old trunks never open
Letting out grey flapping things at twilight?
If it is all as safe and dull
As it seems?

Why then is the stair so steep,
Why is the doorway always locked,
Why does nobody ever come?

THE CALENDAR IN THE ATTIC

I wonder how long it has been
Since this old calendar hung here,
With my birthday date upon it,
Nothing else — not a word of writing —
Not a mark of any hand.

Perhaps it was my father
Who left it thus
For me to see.

Perhaps my mother
Smiled as she saw it;
But in later years did not smile.

If I could tear it down,
From the wall
Somehow
I would be content.
But I am afraid, as a little child, to touch it.

THE ATTIC

THE HOOPSKIRT

In the night when all are sleeping,
Up here a tiny old dame comes tripping,
Looking for her lost hoopskirt.

My great-grandaunt — I never saw her —
Her ghost does n't know me from another,
She stalks up the attic stairs angrily.

The dust sets her sneezing and coughing,
By the trunk she is limping and hopping,
But alas — the trunk is locked.

What 's an old dame to do, anyway!
Must stay in a mouldy grave day on day,
Or go to heaven out of style.

In the night when all are snoring,
The old lady makes a dreadful clatter,
Going down the attic stairs.

What was that? A ghost or a burglar?
Oh, it was only the wind in the chimney,
Yes, and the attic door that slammed.

THE GHOSTS OF AN OLD HOUSE

THE LITTLE CHAIR

I know not why, when I saw the little chair,
I suddenly desired to sit in it.

I know not why, when I sat in the little chair,
Everything changed, and life came back to me.

I am convinced no one at all has grown up in the house,
The break that I dreamed, itself was a dream and is broken.

I will sit in the little chair and wait,
Till the others come looking after me.

And if it is after nightfall they will come,
So much the better.

For the little chair holds me as tightly as death;
And rocking in it, I can hear it whisper strange things.

IN THE DARK CORNER

I brush the dust from this old portrait:
Yes, it is the same face, exactly,
Why does it look at me still with such a look of hate?

THE ATTIC

I brush the dust from a heap of magazines:
Here there is all what you have written,
All that you struggled long years and went down
to darkness for.

O God, to think what I am writing
Will be ever as this!

O God, to think that my own face
May some day glare from this dust!

THE TOY CABINET

By the old toy cabinet,
I stand and turn over dusty things:
Chessmen — card games — hoops and balls —
Toy rifles, helmets, swords,
In the far corner
A doll's tea-set in a box.

Where are you, golden child,
Who gave tea to your dolls and me?
The golden child is growing old,
Further than Rome or Babylon
From you have passed those foolish years.
She lives — she suffers — she forgets.

PART III. THE LAWN

THE THREE OAKS

THERE are three ancient oaks,
That grow near to each other.

They lift their branches
High as beckoning
With outstretched arms,
For some one to come and stand
Under the canopy of their leaves.

Once long ago I remember
As I lay in the very centre,
Between them:
A rotten branch suddenly fell
Near to me.

I will not go back to those oaks:
Their branches are too black for my liking.

THE GHOSTS OF AN OLD HOUSE

AN OAK

Hoar mistletoe
Hangs in clumps
To the twisted boughs
Of this lonely tree.

Beneath its roots I often thought treasure was buried:
For the roots had enclosed a circle.

But when I dug beneath them,
I could only find great black ants
That attacked my hands.

When at night I have the nightmare,
I always see the eyes of ants
Swarming from a mouldering box of gold.

ANOTHER OAK

Poison ivy crawls at its root,
I dare not approach it,
It has an air of hate.

One would say a man had been hanged to its branches,
It holds them in such a way.

THE LAWN

The moon gets tangled in it,
A distant steeple seems to bark
From its belfry to the sky.

Something that no one ever loved,
Is buried here:
Some grey shape of deadly hate,
Crawls on the back fence just beyond.

Now I remember — once I went
Out by night too near this oak,
And a red cat suddenly leapt
From the dark and clawed my face.

THE OLD BARN

Owls flap in this ancient barn
With rotted doors.

Rats squeak in this ancient barn
Over the floors.

Owls flap warily every night,
Rats' eyes gleam in the cold moonlight.

THE LAWN

The moon gets tangled in it,
A distant steeple seems to bark
From its belfry to the sky.

Something that no one ever loved,
Is buried here:
Some grey shape of deadly hate,
Crawls on the back fence just beyond.

Now I remember — once I went
Out by night too near this oak,
And a red cat suddenly leapt
From the dark and clawed my face.

THE OLD BARN

Owls flap in this ancient barn
With rotted doors.

Rats squeak in this ancient barn
Over the floors.

Owls flap warily every night,
Rats' eyes gleam in the cold moonlight.

THE GHOSTS OF AN OLD HOUSE

There is something hidden in this barn,
With barred doors.

Something the owls have torn,
And the rats scurry with over the floors.

THE WELL

The well is not used now,
Its waters are tainted.

I remember there was once a man went down
To clean it.
He found it very cold and deep,
With a queer niche in one of its sides,
From which he hauled forth buckets of bricks and dirt.

THE TREES

When the moonlight strikes the tree-tops,
The trees are not the same.

I know they are not the same,
Because there is one tree that is missing,
And it stood so long by another,
That the other, feeling lonely,
Now is slowly dying too.

THE LAWN

When the moonlight strikes the tree-tops
That dead tree comes back;
Like a great blue sphere of smoke
Half buoyed, half ravelling on the grass,
Rustling through frayed branches,
Something eerily cheeping through it,
Something creeping through its shade.

VISION

You who flutter and quiver
An instant
Just beyond my apprehension;
Lady,
I will find the white orchid for you,
If you will but give me
One smile between those wayward drifts of hair.

I will break the wild berries that loop themselves over
the marsh-pool,
For your sake,
And the long green canes that swish against each other,
I will break, to set in your hands.
For there is no wonder like to you,
You who flutter and quiver
An instant
Just beyond my apprehension.

EPILOGUE

WHY it was I do not know,
But last night I vividly dreamed
Though a thousand miles away,
That I had come back to you.

The windows were the same:
The bed, the furniture the same,
Only there was a door where empty wall had
  always been,
And someone was trying to enter it.

I heard the grate of a key,
An unknown voice apologetically
Excused its intrusion just as I awoke.

But I wonder after all
If there was some secret entrance-way,
Some ghost I overlooked, when I was there.

SECTION II

SYMPHONIES

BLUE SYMPHONY

I

THE darkness rolls upward.
The thick darkness carries with it
Rain and a ravel of cloud.
The sun comes forth upon earth.

Palely the dawn
Leaves me facing timidly
Old gardens sunken:
And in the gardens is water.

Sombre wreck — autumnal leaves;
Shadowy roofs
In the blue mist,
And a willow-branch that is broken.

Oh, old pagodas of my soul, how you glittered
across green trees!

Blue and cool:
Blue, tremulously,
Blow faint puffs of smoke

Across sombre pools.
The damp green smell of rotted wood;
And a heron that cries from out the water.

II

Through the upland meadows
I go alone.
For I dreamed of someone last night
Who is waiting for me.

Flower and blossom, tell me, do you know of her?

Have the rocks hidden her voice?
They are very blue and still.

Long upward road that is leading me,
Light hearted I quit you,
For the long loose ripples of the meadow-grass
Invite me to dance upon them.

Quivering grass
Daintily poised
For her foot's tripping.

Oh, blown clouds, could I only race up like you,
Oh, the last slopes that are sun-drenched and steep!

Look, the sky!
Across black valleys
Rise blue-white aloft
Jagged unwrinkled mountains, ranges of death.

Solitude. Silence.

III

One chuckles by the brook for me:
One rages under the stone.
One makes a spout of his mouth
One whispers — one is gone.

One over there on the water
Spreads cold ripples
For me
Enticingly.

The vast dark trees
Flow like blue veils
Of tears
Into the water.

Sour sprites,
Moaning and chuckling,
What have you hidden from me?

"In the palace of the blue stone she lies forever
Bound hand and foot."

Was it the wind
That rattled the reeds together?

Dry reeds,
A faint shiver in the grasses.

IV

On the left hand there is a temple:
And a palace on the right-hand side.
Foot passengers in scarlet
Pass over the glittering tide.

Under the bridge
The old river flows
Low and monotonous
Day after day.

I have heard and have seen
All the news that has been:
Autumn's gold and Spring's green!

Now in my palace
I see foot passengers

Crossing the river:
Pilgrims of autumn
In the afternoons.

Lotus pools:
Petals in the water.
These are my dreams.

For me silks are outspread.
I take my ease, unthinking.

V

And now the lowest pine-branch
Is drawn across the disk of the sun.
Old friends who will forget me soon,
I must go on,
Towards those blue death-mountains
I have forgot so long.

In the marsh grasses
There lies forever
My last treasure,
With the hopes of my heart.

The ice is glazing over,
Torn lanterns flutter,
On the leaves is snow.

SYMPHONIES

In the frosty evening
Toll the old bell for me
Once, in the sleepy temple.

Perhaps my soul will hear.

Afterglow:
Before the stars peep
I shall creep out into darkness.

SOLITUDE IN THE CITY

(*Symphony in Black and Gold*)

I

WORDS AT MIDNIGHT

BECAUSE the night is so still,
Because there is no one about,
Not the tiny squeak of a mouse over the carpet,
Nor the slow beat of a clock at the top of the stairway,
I am afraid of the night that is coming to me.

I know out there
Some one is thinking of me, some one is wondering about
me,
Some one is needing me, some one is dying for my sake,
Yet I remain alone.

I know that life is calling: I cannot resist it:
Too much of myself I have given ever to turn away,
I know that shame, sickness, death itself shall befall me,
And I am afraid.

O night, hide me in your long cold arms:
Let me sleep, but let me not live this life!

There are too many people with haggard eyes standing
before me
Saying, "To live you must suffer even as we."

Yet life bitterly bids me: "Go on to the last,
No matter the mud and the cold rain and the darkness:
No matter the drear pilgrims in whose eyes you shall look
for long,
And see all suffering, madness, death and despair."

Because my heart is cramped in,
Because I have suffered much,
Because my hope is like a candle-flame quenched at
midnight,
Because I dare dream yet of joy,
I can take my night and the life that is coming to me.

II

THE EVENING RAIN

O the rain of the evening is an infinite thing,
As it slowly slips on the motionless pavement;
Greasy and grey is the rain of the evening,
As it dribbles into the dirty gutters
And slides down the drains with a roar!

SOLITUDE IN THE CITY

Ragged men cower
Under the doorways:
Umbrellas nod like drowsy birds.
Bat-umbrellas,
Teetering, balancing,
Where will you spread your wings to-night?

Tangled between the factory-chimneys,
I have seen the golden lamps wake this evening:
Spinning and whirling, darting and dancing,
Tangled with the glittering rain.

Omnibuses lurch
Heavily homeward
Elephants tinselled in tawdry gold:
Taxicabs fight
Like wild birds squalling,
Wild birds with roaring, clattering wings.

O the rain of the evening is an infinite thing,
As it shivers to jewel-heaps spilt on the pavement.
The façades frown gloomily at its beauty,
The façades are dreaming of the day.

With rippling, curling,
Serpentine convolutions

The pavements drip with drunken light.
Crimson and gold,
Shot with opal,
They glare against the sullen night.

O the rain of the evening is an infinite thing
As it slowly dries on the dirty pavement.
Red low-browed clouds jut over the sky:
And in the cool sky there are stars.

III

STREET OF SORROWS

You street of sorrows bending
Over your golden lamps in the evening;
Dark street that is very silent,
And everywhere the same:
Elsewhere there is song and riot,
Like golden fireflies flickering,
Elsewhere the crane's gaunt muscles
Tug the city up to the stars.

But who in the dawn should come near you?
There are dry leaves rattling behind him.
And who should come in the noonday?
There are shadows that squat on the pave.

SOLITUDE IN THE CITY

And who should come in the evening?
There is one: a ship in dark waters.
And who should come at nightfall,
To feel cold hands at his heart?

You street of solitude waiting
Patient and still in the evening:
Old street that is very weary,
And everywhere the same;
You that have seen joy passing.
Into pain, into tears, into darkness,
Street of the dead and musty,
I have drunk your cold poison to-night.

IV

SONG IN THE DARKNESS

It is the last night that I can be solitary:
Henceforth the keys and wards of me are held in
other hands.

Dark clouds trail over the sky:
Troops of song retreating:
But in the sunset
Once more have I seen aloft
Incredible summits of gold, far on the south horizon.

SYMPHONIES

One purple veil of rain
Floats downward over the city;
And as it settles slowly
The light goes out of it.

Chimneys with massive summits
Stand gaunt and black and evil:
Like a river of lead, to seaward
The river steadily rolls.

It is the last night that I can be solitary:
Life takes me in black coils.

One green light glitters:
Then a swift taxi
Scatters another
As it speeds on.

The chimneys rank
Their motionless forces
Against the swift movement
Of tugs in the stream;
Against the flame-chariots
Of the Embankment;
Against the bowing trees,

SOLITUDE IN THE CITY

Against the blowing smoke,
Against the busy rain.

With dying might
The light invades
The city's hall:
Curtained by dripping fringes
Of buoyant tattered cloud,
Tossed by the wind.

It is the last night that I can be solitary;
And all my city of dreams is burning up to-night.

But yet there waits for me something lost back in the darkness:
Something I have never seized: a shape, a voice, a gesture,
Something behind my shoulder: grey robes that stir and rustle.
Something that moves away from me when I would touch it with my hand.

Cities of the beyond, what great black-walled horizons
Dare you climb up, and down what steep incredible valleys?
I suddenly perceive that I have been mocked in you,
And therefore will I sow the earth with rain of stars to-night.

SYMPHONIES

It is the last night that I can be solitary ;
The rain invites to drunkenness: the wind blows
        through my brain.

Shiplike the sliding golden trams
Procession by and intercross :
With tulips, daffodils, crocuses
The whole street blossoms at my feet:
Now kindle, flames, and let blow out
The crimson rose against the grey,
Let night itself be blotted out
In life's monotonous drone of day.

It is the last night that I can be solitary:
It is the last time that no feet
But mine can beat upon the floor;
It is the last time that no hands
But mine can pound upon my heart ;
It is the last time that no voice
But mine can cry and yet be lost;
It is the last time I shall see
The pavements like a mirror stare at me.

GREEN SYMPHONY

I

THE glittering leaves of the rhododendrons
Balance and vibrate in the cool air;
While in the sky above them
White clouds chase each other.

Like scampering rabbits,
Flashes of sunlight sweep the lawn;
They fling in passing
Patterns of shadow,
Golden and green.

With long cascades of laughter,
The mating birds dart and swoop to the turf:
'Mid their mad trillings
Glints the gay sun behind the trees.

Down there are deep blue lakes:
Orange blossom droops in the water.

In the tower of the winds,
All the bells are set adrift:

SYMPHONIES

Jingling
For the dawn.

Thin fluttering streamers
Of breeze lash through the swaying boughs,
Palely expectant
The earth receives the slanting rain.

I am a glittering raindrop
Hugged close by the cool rhododendron.
I am a daisy starring
The exquisite curves of the close-cropped turf.

The glittering leaves of the rhododendron
Are shaken like blue-green blades of grass,
Flickering, cracking, falling:
Splintering in a million fragments.

The wind runs laughing up the slope
Stripping off handfuls of wet green leaves,
To fling in peoples' faces.
Wallowing on the daisy-powdered turf,
Clutching at the sunlight,
Cavorting in the shadow.

GREEN SYMPHONY

Like baroque pearls,
Like cloudy emeralds,
The clouds and the trees clash together;
Whirling and swirling,
In the tumult
Of the spring,
And the wind.

II.

The trees splash the sky with their fingers,
A restless green rout of stars.

With whirling movement
They swing their boughs
About their stems:
Planes on planes of light and shadow
Pass among them,
Opening fanlike to fall.

The trees are like a sea;
Tossing;
Trembling,
Roaring,
Wallowing,
Darting their long green flickering fronds up at the sky,
Spotted with white blossom-spray.

SYMPHONIES

The trees are roofs:
Hollow caverns of cool blue shadow,
Solemn arches
In the afternoons.
The whole vast horizon
In terrace beyond terrace,
Pinnacle above pinnacle,
Lifts to the sky
Serrated ranks of green on green.

They caress the roofs with their fingers,
They sprawl about the river to look into it;
Up the hill they come
Gesticulating challenge:
They cower together
In dark valleys;
They yearn out over the fields.

Enamelled domes
Tumble upon the grass,
Crashing in ruin
Quiet at last.

The trees lash the sky with their leaves,
Uneasily shaking their dark green manes.

GREEN SYMPHONY

III

Far let the voices of the mad wild birds be calling me,
I will abide in this forest of pines.

When the wind blows
Battling through the forest,
I hear it distantly,
The crash of a perpetual sea.

When the rain falls,
I watch silver spears slanting downwards
From pale river-pools of sky,
Enclosed in dark fronds.

When the sun shines,
I weave together distant branches till they enclose
mighty circles,
I sway to the movement of hooded summits,
I swim leisurely in deep blue seas of air.

I hug the smooth bark of stately red pillars
And with cones carefully scattered
I mark the progression of dark dial-shadows
Flung diagonally downwards through the afternoon.

SYMPHONIES

This turf is not like turf:
It is a smooth dry carpet of velvet,
Embroidered with brown patterns of needles and cones.
These trees are not like trees:
They are innumerable feathery pagoda-umbrellas,
Stiffly ungracious to the wind,
Teetering on red-lacquered stems.

In the evening I listen to the winds' lisping,
While the conflagrations of the sunset flicker and clash behind me,
Flamboyant crenellations of glory amid the charred ebony boles.

In the night the fiery nightingales
Shall clash and trill through the silence:
Like the voices of mermaids crying
From the sea.

Long ago has the moon whelmed this uncompleted temple.
Stars swim like gold fish far above the black arches.

Far let the timid feet of dawn fly to catch me:
I will abide in this forest of pines:
For I have unveiled naked beauty,

GREEN SYMPHONY

And the things that she whispered to me in the darkness,
Are buried deep in my heart.

Now let the black tops of the pine-trees break like a spent
wave,
Against the grey sky:
These are tombs and memorials and temples and altars
sun-kindled for me.

GOLDEN SYMPHONY

I

SEEN from afar, the city
To-day is like a golden cloud:
Strayed from the sky and moulded
Into dim motionless towers.

Music is passing far off:
Music serenely
Is climbing up and vanishing
On the long grey stairways of the sky,
In fanlike rays of light.

Now it falls slowly,
Careering, toppling,
Shivering and quivering like burnished glass or
laburnum-blossom,
Golden cascades.

Peace: now let the music
Sound from further away,
Red bells out of memory's
Blue dream of regret.

GOLDEN SYMPHONY

Seen from afar, the city
To-day is like a fleet of sails:
Breaking the foam of dark forests,
In which I have strayed so long.

They march together slowly,
The golden temple terraces,
Against the dark remembrance
Of my pools of despair.

O golden angelus that sounded prolonging uncertain
memories,
I have seen the swallows hovering to you and followed
their dark trails of passage.

The gates of the city lie open,
And the whole world goes homeward,
Full-pulsing bells in the foreground,
Catching my soul with them
On where the sun soars broadly through the incense-
dome of the sky.

II

High chimes from the belfry;
The noonday approaches

With its golden apparel
Rustling about its feet.

High dreams of my city,
Where we, a band of brothers,
Build our proud dream of beauty
Before we fall into dust.

The golden days have come for us:
With mandolins, sword-thrusts, laughter.
Even the very dust of the street
Grows gold beneath our feet.

Bronze bell-notes poured from deep blue wells:
Molten gold out of the sky.
Pillars of yellow marble
On the summits of which the gods sleep.

Now we are swimming;
About us a great golden halo
Vibrates from us downwards,
Ebbing its life away.

Golden clouds are circling
Like angels and archangels
About the eye of the sun.

Flaming sunset:
Mad conflagrations
Licking at the earth,
The blue-black walls of space,
Iron mountains vast on the horizon.

O golden spear that dartled through the darkness!
The evening star sparkled and threw us its message.

III

In the bosom of the desert
I will lie at the last.

Not the grey desert of sand
But the golden desert of great wild grasses,
This shall receive my soul.

In the high plateaus,
The wind will be like a flute-note calling me
Day after day.

Short bursts of surf,
The wind climbs up and stops in the grass;
And the golden petals
Brush drowsily over my face.

White butterfly that flutters across my sea of golden blossom;
Tell me, what are you looking for, lone white butterfly?

I am seeking for a strange lonely white flower;
Its petals are honeyless; and in the wind it is still.

White butterfly, come, fold your wings over my heart:
I am the white blossom, the white dead blossom for you.

In the golden bosom of the prairie,
I am lying at the last
Like a pool that is stilled.

But they who shared with me my life's adventure,
Who tossed their ducats like dandelions into the sunlight,
I know that somewhere they with songs are building,
Golden towers more beautiful than my own.

IV

I only know in the midnight,
Something will be born of me.

The village drowses in the darkness,
But aloft in the temple
There is a thud of gongs and a shuffle of hollow voices
In the dark corridors.

GOLDEN SYMPHONY

The golden temple
That kindled like a rose against the sunset,
Now is dark and silent,
One light glimmers from its façade.

In the inner shrine
One stiff golden curtain
Hangs from floor to roof.

Black, impassive, helmeted
In felt like stiff black warriors,
The lamas slowly gather,
Kneeling in a row.

The hollow brazen trumpets
Blare and snore.
The drums, festooned with skulls,
Roar.

Suddenly with a clash of gongs,
And a squeal from ear-splitting bugles,
The golden veil is rent.

Cavernous blue darkness!
And within it
Smiling,

SYMPHONIES

Naked,
Rose-empurpled,
Rippling with crimson-violet light, behold the god.

Hail, great jewel in the lotus blossom!
Rosy flame that kindling
Flashes on the emptiness
Or Nirvana's sea!

Before the shrine, as before,
Once more the golden curtain,
And the black shapes vanish.

Aloft in the hollow temple
There is a shuffle of feet and a sound of hollow voices,
Soon lost.

The village drowses in the darkness:
Like a vast black cube
The temple looms above it,
There is no light on its façade.

Suddenly, all the golden temple
Kindles like a rose against the dawn.

I only know in the midnight
Something has been born of me.

WHITE SYMPHONY

I

FORLORN and white,
Whorls of purity about a golden chalice,
Immense the peonies
Flare and shatter their petals over my face.

They slowly turn paler,
They seem to be melting like blue-grey flakes of ice,
Thin greyish shivers
Fluctuating mid the dark green lance-thrust of the leaves.

Like snowballs tossed,
Like soft white butterflies,
The peonies poise in the twilight.
And their narcotic insinuating perfume
Draws me into them
Shivering with the coolness,
Aching with the void.
They kiss the blue chalice of my dreams
Like a gesture seen for an instant and then lost forever.

* *
*

SYMPHONIES

Outwards the petals
Thrust to embrace me,
Pale daggers of coldness
Run through my aching breast.

Outwards, still outwards,
Till on the brink of twilight
They swirl downwards silently,
Flurry of snow in the void.

Outwards, still outwards,
Till the blue walls are hidden,
And in the blinding white radiance
Of a whirlpool of clouds, I awake.

* *
*

Like spraying rockets
My peonies shower
Their glories on the night.

Wavering perfumes,
Drift about the garden;
Shadows of the moonlight,
Drift and ripple over the dew-gemmed leaves.

WHITE SYMPHONY

Soar, crash, and sparkle,
Shoal of stars drifting
Like silver fishes,
Through the black sluggish boughs.

Towards the impossible,
Towards the inaccessible,
Towards the ultimate,
Towards the silence,
Towards the eternal,
These blossoms go.

The peonies spring like rockets in the twilight,
And out of them all I rise.

II

Downwards through the blue abyss it slides,
The white snow-water of my dreams,
Downwards crashing from slippery rock
Into the boiling chasm :
In which no eye dare look, for it is the chasm of death.

Upwards from the blue abyss it rises,
The chill water-mist of my dreams ;
Upwards to greyish weeping pines,
And to skies of autumn ever about my heart,

SYMPHONIES

It is blue at the beginning,
And blue-white against the grey-greenness;
It wavers in the upper air,
Catching unconscious sparkles, a rainbow-glint of sunlight,
And fading in the sad depths of the sky.

Outwards rush the strong pale clouds,
Outwards and ever outwards;
The blue-grey clouds indistinguishable one from another:
Nervous, sinewy, tossing their arms and brandishing,
Till on the blue serrations of the horizon
They drench with their black rain a great peak of change-
less snow.

* *
*

As evening came on, I climbed the tower,
To gaze upon the city far beneath:
I was not weary of day; but in the evening
A white mist assembled and gathered over the earth
And blotted it from sight.

But to escape:
To chase with the golden clouds galloping over the horizon:
Arrows of the northwest wind
Singing amid them,
Ruffling up my hair!

WHITE SYMPHONY

As evening came on the distance altered,
Pale wavering reflections rose from out the city,
Like sighs or the beckoning of half-invisible hands.
Monotonously and sluggishly they crept upwards
A river that had spent itself in some chasm,
And dwindled and foamed at last at my weary feet.

Autumn! Golden fountains,
And the winds neighing
Amid the monotonous hills:
Desolation of the old gods,
Rain that lifts and rain that moves away;
In the green-black torrent
Scarlet leaves.

It was now perfectly evening:
And the tower loomed like a gaunt peak in mid-air
Above the city: its base was utterly lost.
It was slowly coming on to rain,
And the immense columns of white mist
Wavered and broke before the faint-hurled spears.

I will descend the mountains like a shepherd,
And in the folds of tumultuous misty cities,
I will put all my thoughts, all my old thoughts, safely
    to sleep.

SYMPHONIES

For it is already autumn,
O whiteness of the pale southwestern sky!
O wavering dream that was not mine to keep!

* *
*

In midnight, in mournful moonlight,
By paths I could not trace,
I walked in the white garden,
Each flower had a white face.

Their perfume intoxicated me: thus I began my dream.

I was alone; I had no one to guide me,
But the moon was like the sun:
It stooped and kissed each waxen petal,
One after one.

Green and white was that garden: diamond rain hung in the branches,
You will not believe it!

In the morning, at the dayspring,
I wakened, shivering; lo,
The white garden that blossomed at my feet
Was a garden hidden in snow.

It was my sorrow to see that all this was a dream.

WHITE SYMPHONY

III

Blue, clogged with purple,
Mists uncoil themselves:
Sparkling to the horizon,
I see the snow alone.

In the deep blue chasm,
Boats sleep under gold thatch;
Icicle-like trees fret
Faintly rose-touched sky.

Under their heaped snow-eaves,
Leaden houses shiver.
Through thin blue crevasses,
Trickles an icy stream.

The pines groan white-laden,
The waves shiver, struck by the wind;
Beyond from treeless horizons,
Broken snow-peaks crawl to the sea.

* *
*

Wearily the snow glares,
Through the grey silence, day after day,
Mocking the colourless cloudless sky
With the reflection of death.

SYMPHONIES

There is no smoke through the pine tops,
No strong red boatmen in pale green reeds,
No herons to flicker an instant,
No lanterns to glow with gay ray.

No sails beat up to the harbour,
With creaking cordage and sailors' song.
Somnolent, bare-poled, indifferent,
They sleep, and the city sleeps.

Mid-winter about them casts,
Its dreary fortifications:
Each day is a gaunt grey rock,
And death is the last of them all.

* *
*

Over the sluggish snow,
Drifts now a pallid weak shower of bloom;
Boredom of fresh creation,
Death-weariness of old returns.

White, white blossom,
Fall of the shattered cups day on day:
Is there anything here that is not ancient,
That has not bloomed a thousand years ago?

WHITE SYMPHONY

Under the glare of the white-hot day,
Under the restless wind-rakes of the winter,
White blossom or white snow scattered,
And beneath them, dark, the graves.

Dark graves never changing,
White dream drifting, never changing above them:
O that the white scroll of heaven might be rolled up,
And the naked red lightning thrust at the smouldering
earth!

MIDSUMMER DREAMS

(Symphony in White and Blue)

I

THERE is a tall white weed growing at the top
of this sand hill:
In the grass
It is very still.

It lifts its heavy bracts of flattened bloom
Against the sky
Hazily grey with brume.

Out over yonder boats pass
And the swallows
Flatten themselves on the grass.

The lake is silvering beneath the heat.
The wind's feet
Touch lazily each crest,
Like white gulls slow flapping
To windward.

One rose white cloud slowly disengages, loosening itself,
And stands
Above the larkspur-coloured water:
Like Dione's daughter
Braiding up her wet hair with her pale hands.

II

The moon puts out her face at a rift between the trees,
Which do not lift one drooping leaf, this night of June.
There is no lazy breeze to set them clashing adrift.

Thin gleams of silver rise and break in the air,
Fireflies—here and there.

Forest of blue masses suddenly quivering with rapid points
of white,
Are the forests beneath the sea where no breeze passes
As still as you to-night?

The moon puts out her face at a rift between the trees;
Through my window, the bed cut evenly with diagonal
shafts of light,
Is a boat rocking out adrift.

Under it bend the silver tips of the dark blue coral trees,
And fireflies like glass fish
Drift and ripple upwards in the breeze.

III

We are drifting slowly, you and I,
To where the clouds are lifting
High-fretted towers in the sky:
Palaces of ivory,
Which we look at dreamily.
Over our sail
Frail white clouds,
Drift as slowly
Over the undulant pale blue silk of the water,
As we.

We are racing swiftly, you and I,
The sun darts one firm track
Through the blue-black
Of the crinkled water.
Gold spirals spattering, flashing,
The water heaves and curls away at our bow,
A mad fish splashing.

We are rocked together, you and I,
To this undulant movement.
White cloud with blue water blent,
Cloud dipping down to wave its lazy head,

Wave curling under cloud its cloudy blue.
I and you,
All alone, alone, at last.
I hold you fast.

IV

The midsummer clouds were piling up upon the south horizon,
Mountains of drifting translucence in the larkspur-fields of the sky:
Ascending and toppling in crumbled ravines, dribbling down chasms of silence,
Reassembling in crowded multitudes, massive forms one above another.
And I saw in their ridges and hollows, the appearance of a woman
Immeasurable, carven in stainless marble, motionless, naked, fair:
Her head thrown back, her pointed breasts up-gleaming in chill sunlight,
Her heavy flanks dark in the shadow, resting forever inert.
And up to her there suddenly clomb and hurried another cloud,
Huge, hairy, bulging, and knobby, with dark and knotted brows:

And he thrust out long bungling arms to her and drew
himself up to her,
And I watched them melting together, blue mouth to sad
white mouth.

ORANGE SYMPHONY

I

Now that all the world is filled
With armies clamouring;
Now that men no longer live and die, one by one,
But in vague indeterminate multitudes:

Now that the trees are coppery towers,
Now that the clouds loom southward,
Now that the glossy creeper
Spatters the walls like spilt wine:

I will go out alone,
To catch strong joy of solitude
Where the treelines, in gold and scarlet,
Swing strong grape-cables up the smouldering face
of the hill.

II

Guns crashing,
Thudding,
Ululating,
Tumultuous.

SYMPHONIES

Guns yelping over the cracked earth,
Where dry bugles blare.

Here in this hollow
It is very quiet,
Only the wind's hissing laughter
In the place of tombs.

One by one these gaunt scarred faces
Lift up blurred wrinkled inscriptions
Silently beseeching me to stop and ponder.
What does it matter if I do not stop to read them?
No one at all has gone this way that I have chosen before.

A leaf drops slowly in silence ;
It is a long time twisting and hovering on its way to
    the earth.

Guns booming,
Bellowing,
Crashing,
Desperate.
Insistent outcry of savage guns,
Rocking the gloomy hollow.

I will run out like the wind,
Snarling, with savage laughter ;

ORANGE SYMPHONY

Like the wind that tosses the grey-black clouds,
Against the shot-racked barrier of flaming trees.

I will race between the grey guns,
And the clouds, like shrapnel exploding,
Flinging their hail through the tumult,
Bursting, will melt in cold spray.

I am the wanderer of the world;
No one can hold me.
Not the cannon assembled for battle,
Nor the gloomy graves of the hollow,
Nor the house where I long time slumbered,
Nor the hilltop where roads are straggling.
My feet must march to the wind.

Like a leaf dropping slowly,
An orange butterfly turning and twisting,
I touch with moist passionate palms the leaden inscriptions
Of my past. Then I turn to depart.

III

The trees dance about the inn;
The wind thrusts them into flamelets.
Now my thoughts gipsying,
Go forth to strange walls and new fires.

Mouths stained with brown-red berries,
Bronzed cheeks sunken, unshaven,
Ragged attire ;
We swing our guitars at the hip
As we tramp heedless, uncaring.

In the inn the fire crackles :
On the hearth the wine is simmering.
Lift up the brown beaker one instant,
Drink deeply — fling out the last coin — let us go.
On the plains there is drooping harvest,
But no harvest can for long time hold us,
We have seen the winds, baffled,
Racing up the orange-flecked trench of the hills.

IV

On the hill summit
Where the gusty wind all night long has assailed me,
Now I see stars vanishing
Before the long cold clutching fingers of dawn.

Stars scintillant, fire-hued, metallic,
Topaz fruit of the deep-blue garden :
Southward you go, my constellations,
And leave me with the white day, alone.

ORANGE SYMPHONY

Over the hilltop
Swish with a scurry of wings
Millions of pale brown birds,
Songless, pulsing southward.

Birds who have filled the trees,
And who fled long ago at my passing,
Now you clatter in heedless tumult,
Fanning with your hot wings my face.

Carry this word to the southward;
Say that I have forgotten them that wait for me,
All the loves and the hates need expect me no longer,
In the autumn at last I am alone.

Suddenly
The wind crashes through the tree-tops,
Stripping away their orange-tiled domes;
Stark blue skeletons, forbidding
Gesticulate in my face.
You whom I planted and lavished
With all the wealth and beauty I had to bestow
Hurry away, vain harvest,
The winds' scythes can reap you,
Where you lie on the earth, and to death's barns you can go.

Beyond the hilltop
I have seen only the sky.
The wind, naked, prodding up black-furred clouds,
Cossacks of winter.

Cry, wind,
Shriek to the shivering southland,
That I am going into winter,
That I do not hope to return.

Farewell, crowded stars,
Farewell, birds, winds, clouds and treetops,
I, weary of you all, seek my destined joy in the north-
land,
Amid blue ice and the rose-purple night of the pole.

V

Beyond the land there lies the sea;
And on the sea with wings unfurled,
Bloodily huge the sunset rests,
Feathers flickering and claws curled,
Watching to seize the ruined world.

Rolling in a torrent,
Brown leaves, my achievements,
Rise up from dark-wooded valleys

And scatter themselves on the sea;
Brown birds, my wild dreams,
Mingle their bodies together,
Shrieking and clamouring as they pass,
Black charred silhouettes
Against the west, curtained in orange flame.
Now the wind starts up
And strikes the seething water:
Hissing in uncoiled fury
Each foam-curled wave darts forward
To clash and batter
The smouldering iron-rust cliff,
Where the end of my road is lost.

Rise up, black clouds;
Pounce upon the sunset:
Tear it with your jagged teeth.
Fling yourselves, seething winds, in circles
Upon the blue-black water,
Swirl, leaves, and dance
Amid the chaos of breakers,
Flicker, birds, an instant
Against the tawny tiger throat of the sun
Which is snarling in the west.
Beat down, O great winds, westward,
Loose reins and gallop to seaward,

SYMPHONIES

Rush me, too, to that ocean,
In which I have found my goal.

Lash me, lap me, rugged waves of blue-black water,
Dash me, clutch me and do not let me rest one instant;
All through the purple-blue night rock and soothe me,
Till I awaken dreamingly at the faint rose breast of the dawn.

RED SYMPHONY

I

OVER the ink-black cauldron of the sea,
Heavily, on wings of leaden cloud,
Howling the sunset
Races out to assail me.

Long have I voyaged,
Night after night the grey rains swept the sea:
The heaving breakers
Hissed and quivered but held no light.

Now my voyage is ending,
White storm winds have swept bare my soul;
With their harsh laughter,
Their maddening mockery,
Their bayonet-thrusts of despair.

Over the keen, clean-swept zenith
Roll crushingly, huge masses of cloud:
Dull, ponderous, sagging with the burden
Of creaking snow.

SYMPHONIES

They drop flat on the sea,
They hang menacing over me,
They festoon the sun
With swags of crimson light.

They stripe the horizon,
They bar every way with their iron tongues;
They loom weltering over my effort,
They steadfastly close me in.

Meanwhile the sun
With dying force
Wrenches one little crack
In the midst of the sagging masses,
And I steer on to it.

Like a crimson lake
The light overflows and touches the bulging surfaces
With carmine, with scarlet,
With orange, with vermillion,
With brick red, with bluish purple,
With maroon, with rose, with russet,
With savage green, with snowy blue,
With grey, with ebony, with gold.

RED SYMPHONY

It is the storm of the evening
That races out shrieking
To assail me,
And I hail it.

II

The sky's vast emptiness
Is crowded with fragments colliding,
Ragged, splintered masses
Swirling away to the night.

The volcano of the sun
Has burst and split its crater:
Black slag is hurled to the zenith
Above the red lava-sea.

Black shrivelled, charred fragments
Fall into the scarlet torrent:
Huge tresses of darkness sweep over my face,
Leaving me choking.

The sea is one crimson steaming fire;
Each fanged wavelet
Flickers and dances about the one behind it,
Hungrily licking at the ship.

Fierce whirling swords,
Tossed spear-heads lancelike
Spit and stab, then suddenly fall
Leaving me there
On a rolling summit of flame, facing a gulf of despair.

The ship
Lurches
With ice-crusted prow into the wave-trough;
And rises, rapidly dripping liquid fire,
Long twisted necklaces, that burn out to green frozen chrysolite.

III

Over my head a bell beats: it is midnight.
Perhaps I will live to the dawn.

About me are the mouths of yawning furnaces
And from these scarlet mouths the heat outpours,
And darts and licks its dry tongues at my brain
Till it, too, seems a black shell almost bursting
With the force of flame in it.

Still, wearily, I swing my shovel,
Spattering the black coal over the palates
Of the snoring mouths which rapidly swallow.
There is nothing else to do.

My legs seem melting away in sweat beneath me:
In my body my lungs and heart are fighting for air,
My eyes are seared by the appalling scarlet,
Of the furnaces about me — I scarcely see them —
My shovelfuls fall short with every swing.

Without I hear the battering of the tempest,
The ship is pounded sideways by black immeasurable wave-thrusts,
And rising dizzily again, like a half-senseless fighter,
Is again sent downwards, by those unseen fists.

My shovel rises to the ship's slow recovery,
My shovel shoots out at the smash of toppling masses,
Sometimes I pause and pant for an endless instant,
While the ship crouches, quivering.

Over my head a bell beats: it is morning.
Wearily I drop the shovel,
And drag myself to the deck.

IV

Afar
There is something that seems a shore;
The sky has been blown clean of clouds except to westward,
And these stare hard at me, like huge sardonyx towers.

SYMPHONIES

I cling to a half-shattered rail that reels and dances,
Soused by the choking water,
My face a streaming mass of blood and salt and grime,
I wait and dizzily I try to remember.

What is this city that out there awaits me?
Am I its conqueror?

Will scarlet flags hang fluttering in the streets
To greet my coming?
Will crimson lanterns
Jingle and toss in festival to-night?

Has the fire burned the ship and is the water
But stinging icy fire,
That whips and sears my face?

Down there the furnaces go out, for the water
Sloshes about the floor;
And steaming acrid fumes arise,
No living soul could stay in such a place.

Out here the decks are shattered,
The boats are shorn away,
And far on the horizon,
The city glares with its sardonyx towers.

RED SYMPHONY

Now the red bells,
The black-red bells,
The storm bells,
Break loose from the horizon,
Leaping upon the eastern sea,
And breaking it in their teeth.

The towers
Infuriate, enkindle
From base to summit,
In layers, and orange terraces,
Against the blue snow haze that drifts down on them
from the east.

The ship of my soul
Is rolling to port at last,
With one clang from its heaving boilers,
One sigh from its shaking funnels,
One rattle from its loosened chains.
I will lash myself to the masthead
And wait
Empty-eyed and open-mouthed,
Till the city that is all one scarlet flame of death
Takes me to itself at last.

VIOLET SYMPHONY

I

BUT yesterday
Moonsails were raking high the harbour of my dreams.

Dull night of trees,
Dark sorrows drooping,
Glittering raindrops gleam on you
In recollection
Of my despair.

But yesterday
Stardust was scattered deep on the dark gulf of my dreams.

Wind of the night,
Questing, swaying, calling,
Rustle of dull grasses,
Why do you trouble me?

Yesterday
Purple mist was powdered on the windless sea of dreams.

Faces of the night that pass me,
Haggard, monotonous faces,
Windblown hair and lustful lips,
I am not what you desire.

Yesterday
One — two — sails above the mist —
Windswallows that hover
Towards the rainclouds of the horizon,
Out of the reedy harbours
Rocking, swaying, falling,
Blown to sea and parted
Yesterday,
Yesterday.

II

Purple-blue bloom of night,
Globed grapes clustered morosely
Down the dark vineyards of untrodden streets:

The noise of the moments is like the clash of the hoofs
of a horse rattling,
Thin tattoo in the stillness:
The noise of the moments takes me, uncaring,
Towards the day.

VIOLET SYMPHONY

With brassy crash, dawn's corybants
Invade and trample the vineyard :
Like a faun I hide and watch them,
A dark cup in my hand.

Spoilers of my vineyard,
Spilling the lees of my sweet red wine,
You will yet ask in vain for a cup that is not yours,
A purple, dewy cup of lonely night.

Tramplers in the morning,
Sunburnt faces and weary lips,
There is yet a cup here you cannot have,
I hold it in my hands.

Would you drink of it ?
Lay down your thyrse and timbrel.
Break the harsh dance that flickers through the morning,
Forget the scarlet perfumes of the day.

Remember only starless night, cool swish of many seas.

Faint pearl-glow of evening,
Cool marble in the silence:
Purple-blue grapes of night crushed freshly,
Deep sleep and the drowsy stars.

VIOLET SYMPHONY

III

I love the night that in long violet shroud
Slowly and lovingly wraps up the day,
Hiding its blurred imperfections
In endless tenderness.

I love the day's
High violet cone of light,
With thin haze on the horizon
Like a wavering summer sea.

But most of all I love midsummer dawn,
When far-off planes of light ascend and tremble together
Like distant purple waves, the sound of whose dim breaking
Is lost in the wild babel of awaking birds.

IV

Twisted fragments of violet paper,
The dawn drops you
Into the green bowl filled with the day's grey waves.

I love the night's
Deep purple grapes
That yesterday
Were crushed and spilled,

SYMPHONIES

In long and sluggish rivers
That joined and made a sea,
Where, half-guessed through the mist,
Two golden sails
Drifted on silently.

The blue fume of my dreams
Is laced with violet flame.

One golden sail alone came back to rest
In its nest
Among the reeds.
The other sail is lost;
Behind the mist,
Beyond the craggy rock,
About which race in jagged white
The waves,
Horizon on horizon far away
She waits.
But through the day,
Comes no faint song, nor creaking of the ropes.

Twisted fragments of violet paper,
Charred and fallen:
Out of the green bowl lazily coils grey smoke.

GREY SYMPHONY

I

Up on the hillside a long row of larches
Shake from their grizzled beards the vestiges of rain,
From grey-blue melting ice-slabs 'neath their arches
The spring goes up again.

Writhing, exuding,
Up-steaming, streaming,
The earth is breathing to the sky
Wet clouds of spring.

Dim rosy fans, the trees
As they flick to and fro,
Seem driving greyish vapour
Over the snow.

The sky remodulates itself
From violet-grey to blue,
Under the upturned eaves of the blue larches
The sun looks through.

SYMPHONIES

Now with the heat of the sun
The grey-blue ice-slabs quiver,
They slide in muddy trickles
Towards the river.

Up on the hillside between the long row of larches
Fume up from south pale clouds that bear the rain;
In pearl and violet arches
They break and shape again.

II

I have seen in the evening
The greyish-violet clouds
Roll wearily back from northward
To the place whence first they came.

One or two orange lamps burnt low
Against deep purple hills —

The wind was hurrying, bundling them together,
The pines awoke to sing
The song of the snow buzzing and screaming
On its one string.

I have seen within my heart
Crocuses, purple and gold,

Drop cold and dull and colourless
Beneath the snow.

One or two orange lamps burnt low,
Vain memories.

The wind has driven me too many winters,
My songs are snowflakes whirling about my breast.
I will wrap my frozen and bitter songs about me,
In one grey drift, and rest.

III

Fluttering and soft the snow
Flings outward, swirls and settles,
But when I try to seize it,
The wind tears it away.

Through poised green platforms of enormous pines,
I see far hilltops pushing up blue roofs.
Snow comes,
And hums
Through the woof
Of the lower branches.
It skips and dances:
It drops in sluggish folds
Of grey,

SYMPHONIES

To where the frozen rhododendron bushes
With lower air-gusts play,
And the earth hushes
Its movement.

Fluttering and soft the snow is blent
In long loose spirals with my dream.

It is all I have, the snow,
And I know
That when I chase it, it will fly from me ;
Beyond the lifeless green,
Beyond the low blue hills,
Beyond the pale straw-coloured glare,
Down in the west
It goes ;
Straight southward where the purple-orange flare
Of sunset flows,
And into the blackened heart of my last rose
Pours its despair.

Fluttering, soft, and dim
Regrets that skip and skim
Grey in the grey twilight ;
Slim and weary whirls the snow,
And where it goes I too shall go.

GREY SYMPHONY

IV

Of my long nights afar in alien cities
I have remembered only this:
They were black scarves all dusted over with silver,
In which I wrapped my dreams;
They were black screens on which I made those pictures
That faded out next day.

Youth without glory, manhood one mad struggle,
Maturity a battle without trumpet calls:
Long gleams from pallid suns seen only in my dreaming
Struck those dissolving walls.

And of my days,
I only know
They slipped and fell,
Like too-brief sunsets,
Into the hill-ravines that held the snow.

Three lofty pines
At the corners of my heart
Waited, apart.

SYMPHONIES

They only see
In the mystery
Of the grey sky,
The jaggled clouds that fly,
Endlessly.

POPPIES OF THE RED YEAR

(A Symphony in Scarlet)

I

THE words that I have written
To me become as poppies:
Deep angry disks of scarlet flame full-glowing in the stillness
Of a shut room.

Silken their edges undulate out to me,
Drooping on their hairy stems;
Flaring like folded shawls, down-curved like rockets starting
To break and shatter their light.

Wide-flaunting and heavy, crinkle-lipped blossom,
Darting faint shivers through me;
Globed Chinese lanterns on green silk cords a-swaying
Over motionless pools.

These are lamps of a festival of sleep held each night to
    welcome me,
Crimson-bursting through dark doors.
Out to the dull, blue, heavy fumes of opium rolling
From their rent red hearts, I go to seek my dream.

II

A riven wall like a face half torn away
Stares blankly at the evening:
And from a window like a crooked mouth
It barks at the sunset sky.

And over there, beyond,
On plains where night has settled,
Tent-like encampments of vaporous blue smoke or mist,
Three men are riding.

One of them looks and sees the sky:
One of them looks and sees the earth:
The last one looks and sees nothing at all.
They ride on.

One of them pauses and says, "It is death."
Another pauses and says, "It is life."
The last one pauses and says, "'T is a dream."
His bridle shakes.

The sky
Is filled with oval violet-tinted clouds
Through which the sun long settled strikes at random,
Enkindling here and there blotched circles of rosy light.

These are poppies,
Unclosing immense corollas,
Waving the horsemen on.

Over the earth, upheaving, folding,
They ride : their bridles shake :
One of them sees the sky is red :
One of them sees the earth is dark :
The last man sees he rides to his death,
Yet he says nothing at all.

III

There will be no harvest at all this year ;
For the gaunt black slopes arising
Lift the wrinkled aching furrows of their fields, falling away,
To the rainy sky in vain.

But in the furrows
There is grass and many flowers.
Scarlet tossing poppies
Flutter their wind-slashed edges,
On which gorged black flies poise and sway in drunken sleep.

The black flies hang
Above the tangled trampled grasses,
Grey, crumpled bundles lie in them :

They sprawl,
Heave faintly;
And between their stiffened fingers,
Run out clogged crimson trickles,
Spattering the poppies and standing in beads on the grass.

IV

I saw last night
Sudden puffs of flame in the northern sky.

The sky was an even expanse of rolling grey smoke,
Lit faintly by the moon that hung
Its white face in a dead tree to the east.

Within the depths of greenish greyish smoke
Were roars,
Crackles and spheres of vapour,
And then
Huge disks of crimson shooting up, falling away.

And I said these are flower petals,
Sleep petals, dream petals,
Blown by the winds of a dream.

But still the crimson rockets rose.
They seemed to be

One great field of immense poppies burning evenly,
Casting their viscid perfume to the earth.

The earth is sown with dead,
And out of these the red
Blooms are pushing up, advancing higher,
And each night brings them nigher,
Closer, closer to my heart.

V

By the sluggish canal
That winds between thin ugly dunes,
There are no passing boats with creaking ropes to-day.

But when the evening
Crouches down, like a hurt rabbit,
Under the everlasting raincloud whirling up the north horizon,
Downwards on the stream will float
Glowing points of fire.

Orange, coppery, scarlet,
Crimson, rosy, flickering,
They pass, the lanterns
Of the unknown dead.

Out where the sea, sailless,
Is mouthing and fretting
Its chaos of pebbles and dried sticks by the dunes.

By the wall of that house
That looks like a face half torn away,
And from its flat mouth barks at the sky,
The sky which is shot with broad red disks of light,
Petals drowsily falling.

VI

"It was not for a sacred cause,
Nor for faith, nor for new generations,
That unburied we roll and float
Beneath this flaming tumult of drunken sleep-flowers.
But it was for a mad adventure,
Something we longed for, poisonous, seductive,
That we dared go out in the night together,
Towards the glow that called us,
On the unsown fields of death.

"Now we lie here reaped, ungarnered,
Red swaths of a new harvest:
But you who follow after,
Must struggle with our dream:

And out of its restless and oppressive night,
Filled with blue fumes, dull, choking,
You will draw hints of that vision
Which we hold aloof in silence."

THE END

The Riverside Press
CAMBRIDGE . MASSACHUSETTS
U . S . A